LEARN FROM FEMINA MISS INDIA FINALIST
DIVYA MISRA

SAY IT WITH CONFIDENCE
MASTERING COMMUNICATION IN EVERY SITUATION

BLUEROSE PUBLISHERS
India | U.K.

Copyright © Divya Misra 2025

All rights reserved by author. No part of this publication may be reproduced, stored in a retrieval system or transmitted in any form or by any means, electronic, mechanical, photocopying, recording or otherwise, without the prior permission of the author. Although every precaution has been taken to verify the accuracy of the information contained herein, the publisher assumes no responsibility for any errors or omissions. No liability is assumed for damages that may result from the use of information contained within.

BlueRose Publishers takes no responsibility for any damages, losses, or liabilities that may arise from the use or misuse of the information, products, or services provided in this publication.

For permissions requests or inquiries regarding this publication, please contact:

BLUEROSE PUBLISHERS
www.BlueRoseONE.com
info@bluerosepublishers.com
+91 8882 898 898
+4407342408967

ISBN: 978-93-6452-063-8

Cover Design: Aman Sharma
Typesetting: Pooja Sharma

First Edition: January 2025

Acknowledgements

Writing this book has been one of the most rewarding experiences of my life, and it wouldn't have been possible without the incredible support and encouragement of many wonderful people.

First and foremost, I want to express my deepest gratitude to my family, who loves me unconditionally.

To my parents, who instilled in me the values of perseverance and hard work, and who have always believed in my dreams, even when I doubted them myself.

To my colleagues, who guided me with wisdom and insight throughout this journey. Their advice has shaped not only this book but also my own personal and professional growth.

I am incredibly grateful to my editor and the entire publishing team for their meticulous attention to detail and for helping me bring this vision to life.

Finally, thanks to every reader who picks up this book. It is for you that I have written these pages, and I hope the words inspire, empower, and help you on your journey towards confident communication.

With sincere appreciation,

Divya Misra

Author Introduction

Divya Misra is a former Miss India Delhi Finalist 2014 with over ten years of experience in performing arts. She is a certified actor who has worked in a Gujarati movie, "Romance Complicated" as a lead actress which was released on 15th January 2015. Divya Misra, an actor, model, and anchor is also a professional and a certified voice-over artist. She has also been working as a faculty member in various institutes in Delhi, wherein she has taught students acting, communication skills and personality development. Divya Misra is an ICF (International Coaching Federation) certified trainer, an NLP (Neuro-Linguistic Programming) coach and a certified communication trainer with an aim to transform and enrich the field of communication with her experience.

Foreword

I felt nervous when my daughter, Divya, requested me to write the foreword for her maiden book. While I was overwhelmed by the respect she held for me, at the same time, the moments filled me with excitement for the reason that the subject she had dwelt in her book had been my grey areas which I always strived to overcome. While recalling my school and college days, and for that matter, also the period of my service with the Central Government in various capacities, I feel that the topics covered in the book, beside being indispensable are prerequisite for every student and those aspiring to etch out their place in schools, colleges, the working place, and of course in society as such.

Confidence and communication are closely interwoven skills. lack of one can make it difficult for the other to achieve its objective effectively. On the one hand, people with confidence are considered more assertive during the period of crisis and are likely to express themselves clearly and efficaciously, while on the other hand, people who lack the confidence may avoid speaking up, sharing their views. They may also lack the capacity to understand others perspectives. Presence of these two traits in a person, besides enhancing aura of his overall personality, can help him to stand out in professional settings. It can create a positive and empowering ambience at their workplace, for laying road to the lasting success.

Being the father of a lovely and affectionate daughter, I found her to be a very shy and reserved child during her school days. But, somewhere, she was blessed with the latent potential of making her place on the occasions and when she was exposed to opportunities for it—be it as an actress, model, or communication coach. That exposure was her driving force which prompted her to understand the power of being a confident and an effective communicator through the experiences she gained in the later period of her life.

In her Book, Divya has impressively dwelt on **Confidence and Communication** and their related aspects in a very vivid and effective manner, so much so that the book would deserve to be a permanent part of one's bookshelf. I hope this book will definitely be immensely liked and enjoyed by those who aspire and cherish the goals during periods of their school, colleges, workplaces, and their social circles.

P.k Misra

Father

Preface

I remember getting rejected from the final round of Miss India competition in 2011 because of the lack of communication skills, and then making it to the top 14 state finalists in 2014. I have learned my lessons the hard way and, to be honest, I have worked very hard to become the confident version of myself. In the last 14 years of experiencing and making my way through life, I have learned one of the most important lesson, you are only what you can communicate to the world. If you are not going to tell the world what you want, they will serve you with what is convenient for them. My journey in these years has not been the easiest, but apparently my biggest teacher of all time. As someone who has suffered depression, anxiety, and a lonely childhood, this book is a testament that nobody needs to suffer silently. The power of communication is incredible. You have all the magic inside you to conquer every difficulty and shine like a star that you are. Keep this book with you all the time, so you never fail to communicate to the world that you deserve nothing but the best.

Say it with Confidence- Mastering Communication in Every Situation

---

Chapters

Chapter 1-Understanding Confidence: Foundations for Effective Communication

- Foundation of a confident you
- Self-awareness for effective communication
- The Mindset

Chapter 2 - Mastering Verbal Communication: The Power of Words

- Techniques of speaking confidently
- Clarity in communication
- Be assertive
- Overcome speech-related anxiety.

Chapter 3- Harnessing Non-verbal Communication: Beyond Words

- Body language
- Facial expressions
- Non-verbal signals

Chapter 4 - Building Rapport and Connection: The Heart of Effective Communication

- Strategies for establishing rapport
- Active listening
- Empathetic communication

Chapter -5 Overcoming Fear and Anxiety: Confidence in Challenging Situations

- Managing nervousness
- Handling difficult conversations
- Speaking up in various contexts

Chapter 6 - Developing Assertiveness: Setting Boundaries and Expressing Needs

- How to express opinions
- Saying no respectfully
- Assert boundaries without being aggressive

Chapter 7 - Adapting Communication Styles: Flexibility for Different Audiences

- Importance of flexibility in communication
- Strategies for tailoring messages to diverse listeners

Chapter 8 - Confidence in Public Speaking: Owning the Stage

- Preparing and delivering speeches
- Managing stage fright
- Engaging an audience effectively

Chapter 9-Handling Criticism and Feedback: Turning Challenges into Growth Opportunities

- Constructive ways to receive and respond to feedback
- Turning criticism into opportunities for growth and learning

Chapter 10-Maintaining Confidence Long-Term: Strategies for Sustainable Communication

- Maintaining confidence over time
- Setting communication goals
- Continuing to grow as a confident communicator

Chapter - 1
Understanding Confidence

The foundation of a confident you

When it comes to personal development, one of the biggest mistakes we have been making for ages is not understanding the root cause of the things you are not able to achieve. Confidence is not a technique that can be learned and applied instantly; it is a muscle that takes some time to build and would need everyday practise and dedication. I tell my students all the time, they have spent so many years thinking about the problems, it's high time to start finding the solutions. Confidence is nothing but the art of mastering how you feel about yourself all the time. When was the last time you stopped obsessing over "I don't feel confident" and started asking yourself, "Why do I don't feel confident?" If you just close your eyes right now and honestly ask yourself, you would be surprised that the answer lies within you. Let me tell you one of the biggest reasons why confidence has not knocked on your door yet. Perhaps, you have not started working it out. Let's say you want to be confident on stage. You have been thinking about getting better at this stage for such a long time. My question to you is, how many times in a month have you given yourself the space to do that? I bet your answers is less than five or maybe zero for a lot of you. You, see? If getting better at communication is something that you want to genuinely do, how many times have you gone among people and initiated or had conversations, for that matter, last time? This is what I am talking about, and this is the number one foundation of confidence, i.e., exposure. To become confident at something you must do it repeatedly, till the time it becomes a piece of cake. Either it's the stage, presentations, or saying no. Let's get this one thing out of your head today, the first time you do them, you are going to be dreadful at it. You only get better with time and the amount of time you expose yourself to it. Yes, it's that simple.

This brings me to the second foundation of a confident you, having unrealistic expectations from yourself. Perfectionism is a myth, and as quickly as you would make this your mantra, you would start feeling confident almost instantly. Most of the time, you don't feel your best because you set the bar way too high for yourself. How about I tell you, you are going to keep making mistakes until your last breath you take on this earth, and still, you can be called confident by so many. You may ask how, **"Confident people are not the people who don't make mistakes, they are the people who own them"**.

This brings me to the last foundation of confidence, "Nobody is thinking about you, in fact, most of the people are not even thinking about themselves" I have spoken to hundreds of people and the biggest blockage that has stopped them from feeling good about themselves is what other people are thinking about them. Let me give you an example. You go to see someone speak on stage. Let's say a comedian. Do you start making judgements about them? You may look at the clothes they are wearing or how they are standing, but I am pretty sure the people in the auditorium are looking at that comedian only with the intention of listening to his act. What did we learn here? People are not giving a hoot about anything in general, everything is mostly in your head, and that's something we can work on. You don't need to and can't work on other people's minds or what they are thinking, that's an unreal expectation. What you can work on is yourself, and that's the story that we will unravel in the coming chapters. Becoming a confident communicator is not a rocket science but a science of you, a science of how humans behave and once you master your own game, there is no looking back from there. I hope you have started feeling better.

2-Self-awareness for effective communication

For the longest time, you have kept yourself deprived of this one simple thing – awareness. We see the most confident people in the world and begin doubting our abilities, whether we would ever be able to become that way. Let me tell you a secret, I have been an actor and model for more than eleven years now, and the celebrities that you see who are confident all the time have gone through rigorous self-work journeys before they appeared on screen. What makes them confident is the team that coaches them to talk, walk, and most importantly, the way they carry themselves, their looks. A whole team is behind making them look and feel confident. If you look at the biggest actors' interviews from the last 20 years, you would notice a pattern. They all were mostly terrible in their first interviews. However, later with the passage of time, they sound better, confident, and composed. So, what changed it? You may think, practise and experience, which is 100% right, but what is not tangible to you is the heightened self-awareness.

This brings me to my first point, A. Get to know yourself. Who are you, what are you, what your core beliefs are, what drives you mad, and what makes you happy. When was the last time you checked them out? Let's study this with a realistic example. A very common question that has been asked by so many people, and you must have heard it too. "When was the last time you felt happy?" People answer this question by telling the experiences they had in the past that made them content and joyful. My question to you is, how many times did you try to repeat those same experiences? I bet your answer is not more than once or twice. Now, this is what I am talking about. Life has a million ways to tell you what makes you fulfilled or whole, but if you keep your self-awareness button switched off, how in the world are you going to figure out what makes you, 'YOU'. If you know who you are, the chances of you feeling confident about your decisions are going to increase by 30%.

B. Self-awareness is not only about getting to know yourself, but this is also one of the core elements. Self-awareness helps you to emotionally regulate yourself. Confidence is not an outcome of how many people said, "You look nice", which made you feel good about yourself. Confidence is looking in the mirror and telling yourself "You have got this". When you are self-aware, you know that no matter what people say I am going to believe in my capabilities. Once you are self-aware, you are in absolute control of your emotions, and an external force would not make you doubt yourself at any moment.

C. Adaptability. Once you are fully self-aware and understand how emotions work, you start getting better at flexibility. A lot of times our confidence gets shaky because there is a lot of noise in the environment. People keep saying and doing things that you have never done and tried, which makes you start believing that you are not enough. Once you are self-aware and understand that this journey is not only about learning but also about unlearning, you achieve grace. You become more open to adapting to different perspectives. I am not sure if you have noticed, but a lot of your confidence is stuck in your head, which keeps battling between what is right and what is wrong. We spend so much energy proving each other wrong that we miss realising that confidence and growth come from the area releasing your brain from the fear of being wrong. Let's get this one thing out of your head today. It's better to be proved wrong by an idiot who does not even know what the right is. Don't let those idiots grind you or your confidence down.

3- The mindset shifts

Imagine you are on stage for the very first time. You are going to feel nervous, right? Now imagine ten people in the audience who are shouting your name at the top of their voice saying, "You are Amazing." This is going to bring a smile to your face, and you will instantly feel good about yourself in that very moment. Tell me, in that moment what changed for you? How did you become confident from being nervous? When people started shouting your name the attention shifted from being self-conscious to self-confident. Now imagine doing that with yourself without waiting for people to do it for you. Let's understand this basic thing, every good thing happening to you is just a mindset shift away. Most of our confidence goes down the drain because we fail to shift our mindset from, "what if I fail while doing this" to "I will try my best and accept what it offers" mindset.

Most of the time, we fail to become the best versions of ourselves because we are stunted from such a long time. We have made ourselves believe that I am born a certain way, and I can't change. My role in this life is this, and it can't change. Our lives have been shaped by people around us who have their own self-limiting beliefs. You have not even tried doing certain things because according to the norms of a society it should not be done. Our brains have been developed by the people who have been taught by the people who did not know even a small hint of how life should be lived in a wholesome way. They all may have been following a mob mentality. You have been believing the things that people around you made you believe.

I am here to tell you that you can change every single part about yourself if it is not serving you anymore. I am pretty sure that you have not given enough attention to the part that is not making you happy or, for that matter, confident. From fixed to growth mindset, scarcity to abundance mindset, it's all about changing your perspective. That's one of the most important foundations of becoming confident in yourself.

Remember, before we try to achieve anything in life you must trust yourself that it is achievable. One of the biggest side effects of low self-confidence is that your brain tricks you into believing things that are not true. Your brain has tricked you into believing that you can't feel confident the way you would like and have been wanting, but the reality is it's 110% achievable. We need to build systems for you to be able to build over the course of a few days and months and you will be good to shine at your brightest. Why don't you take a deep breath and write this down on a piece of paper, "I am fully capable of becoming a confident version of myself", and repeat this every morning till you finish this book.

"Confidence is like a superhero cape — it doesn't matter if you're wearing pyjamas underneath; as long as you own it, you're ready to save the day!"

Chapter - 2
Mastering Verbal Communication

Since the time I started teaching communication skills, I have come across one of the biggest barriers amongst students, especially in India. The obsession over speaking in English, students have wasted so much time thinking they are not good at English that it has hampered their basic conversational skills. In this process, we have completely forgotten that communication skills are not only about mastering a language, it's about what you say and more importantly how you say it. For the next ten minutes, I need you to forget about the language and concentrate on what you say all the time.

Let's understand how the logistics work when it comes to mastering your conversational skills. Let me ask you a question. What do you do when you have an exam coming up? You prepare, right? What exactly happens when you attend your examination without preparing for it. You play the guessing game and write whatever you know. The chances of you doing well in the exam decrease drastically. Having a conversation is very similar to preparing for the examination. The more one prepares, the better are the chances for him or her to perform well. From delivering a compelling speech to having a conversation with your dear friend, preparing for it will reduce your anxiety by 70%. Let's understand how to prepare for a casual conversation.

1. **Set an objective** – Can you reach somewhere without knowing the directions to it? We often feel less fulfilled in our friendships and daily conversations with the people we know because we don't set the agenda for it. Imagine you are sitting in a circle of your friends and setting the agenda like, "Today we will discuss how we all are doing when it comes to our mental health." Wouldn't that be easy for everyone to open their hearts and share? Setting an objective for conversations not only gives you a roadmap of what to speak about but also an end goal.

2. **What do you know?** – One of the biggest hindrances for you as a conversationalist is a lack of knowledge. Imagine standing in between people but having nothing to share and talk about. Sounds familiar? My question to you is, do you make a serious effort to widen your knowledge about the things you are interested in? You don't specifically have to have an opinion about what other people are saying, all you need is to have an opinion about the things YOU care about. The idea is to have better self-awareness about the things that you are interested in.

3. **Are you okay?** - Yes, I am fine, and the conversation has ended successfully. You see what happens when you ask questions like, are you okay? Did you like that? Are you bored? You are not giving other people the opportunity to open up and elaborate. For conversations to have meaning is to ask an open-ended question. When a person asks an open-ended question, it gives the other person the opportunity to elaborate on the things they want to speak about. Some of the examples of an open-ended question are "What all happened during your day at work? I am curious."

"How was your weekend? Did you get a chance to relax and unwind?" "Is everything alright with you? Do you want to talk about it?"

4. Do you really care? – Yes, I am asking you. Do you really care about the person you want to have a conversation with? You might say, I try my best to listen, but my attention goes away. When was the last time you asked yourself, "Do I really care about what he or she is saying or am I fooling myself?" In recent times, we have been absorbed so deeply in ourselves and in our lives that we have not paid attention to what is really happening in other people's lives. If you want to have meaningful conversations with people and not feel drained out by the end of it, you need to start caring for real. When you listen, listen with an intention of learning something from their experience and not with "when this person is going to stop blabbering so I can speak." Remember, if your mouth is open, you are not learning.

5. Stop Multitasking- No, this doesn't mean that you are trying to finish work in middle of a conversation, it means, Stay here IN THIS MOMENT. When you are talking to people, stop thinking about random things like "Did I close the bathroom window?" "How am I going to finish the tasks by EOD?" or "I am really getting hungry, what's for lunch?" Your mind going in different directions is pretty much normal, but you must take a deep breath and intentionally try to come back to where you are standing or sitting. One of the biggest problems of juggling between random thoughts when you are communicating is that you miss on important or minute details and then the conversation will start feeling like you really need to escape, which is going to suck out the real essence of it. Eventually, you will come back to where you started "I am not good at making conversations" which we don't want. Better stay in the moment.

6. Okay then? -One of the most difficult parts of having a conversation is that we struggle to interrupt and say that I need to leave. Am I right? I can feel you just nodded your head. Let's understand how to do that. If you follow the above rules of having conversations with people you may end up having a great conversation, but you don't have the bandwidth all the time to spend 30 minutes. Now the trick is to find cues and assure your fellow communicator that this was interesting, and you want to keep having it, but you really must leave for your meeting at work. If you don't always have something to look forward to but if you really need to find a way to say goodbye, then you need to have realistic scenarios up your sleeve. Things like, I have an important meeting at work, or a doctor's appointment. I need to feed my pet at home, etcetera are great ways to interrupt the flow. You can say things like, "Hey, I would love to know more about that spa you went to this Sunday because I have been meaning to go by myself, but I really have to go for this appointment I booked a month ago, shall we continue this tomorrow?" You see? This did not even feel like a goodbye and sounded very polite.

7. Your opinion doesn't matter- Well, it does, I was kidding but not all the time. Tell me, do you share your feelings with your friends? Do you express your opinions regarding any advice you get from them? No right? You share because you want to understand that your feelings are true, and they matter, and you need their support for the same. You will ask for advice if you really want. So, what did we learn here? Stay silent, listen, and hold your temptations by giving some advice all the time. People don't like getting lectured all the time. If you have asked someone a genuine open-ended question and you see them opening up for the same, try to respect that and acknowledge their feelings and emotions with, "I understand how you feel", "I am glad you are happy", "I am sorry you feel this way", or "Thank you for opening up" rather than saying "you are probably right but I feel you need to...." "I get it, but you know this is what I have learnt..."

8. Finish it already - No, not my book but your statements. You start opening but without this realisation that you are stretching the same topic way too long. When talking, especially with new people, try to be brief and concise. Most of the time, people ignore people because they just share things for an extended period. As a listener, if someone hasn't stopped talking for more than 2 minutes it's hard to keep up. Practise talking about your favourite things at home with limited sentences. Prepare the things that you wish to share and don't share more than that. It's a good idea to rewire your brain from "I am going to share it all" to "This should be enough for them." This is one of the best ways to make people attracted towards you as a communicator.

Till that time, making conversation doesn't feel like a task for you, I would highly recommend you keep the **3 Ps in mind. Prepare, Practice, Persevere**. After applying the above tricks, you may still end up messing it all up, but the idea is to keep at it no matter what, and while you do that, don't judge yourself too harshly. Be compassionate and communicate this one line to yourself before you make a conversation. "It's okay if things don't go my way in the beginning, I will not give up and will keep trying."

Chapter - 3
Harnessing Non-verbal Communication, Beyond Words

When was the last time you noticed someone taking a grand entry in a room full of people and creating an impact without speaking a single word? You must have seen celebrities posing for award shows and paparazzi, and looking stunning. So, what do they do which we fail to do and create an impact? Their body language, their non-verbal cues. Non-verbal communication is nothing but when your body is talking as your mouth stays shut. We feel so anxious to even hold a conversation that we have hardly paid any attention to what our body and face are doing when our lips are sealed. Body language and understanding non-verbal cues is an extremely huge topic, so let's make it relatable and easy for you to apply and practise it in your daily life to stand out in the crowd.

One of the biggest fears of human beings when speaking in public is the fear of being perceived or judged in some way by other human beings, which, by the way, you should be least bothered about. But, how about I tell you that people start making judgements about you even before you open your mouth. Our anxiety shows in every possible way in our body, and that's where the real challenge lies. Self-Control. Did you notice yourself doing the following things in public?

1. Cracking fingers
2. Lip smacking.
3. Swaying your hands back and forth
4. Shaking your leg while sitting
5. Moving your body weight side to side in a chair
6. Touching your hair
7. Touching your neck and chin
8. Urge to check your phone to look busy.
9. Crossing your arms and pacifying your arm's by slowly touching it up and down

I am assuming you must have picked 2-3 habits out of these. These are all our anxiety pacifying behaviours and make you perceive less confident in a public setting. While some of these habits are also passed on through genetics including anxiety, some of them are purely to feel normal. Let's visualise something for five seconds. Close your eyes and visualise yourself among a bunch of people doing absolutely nothing, and then imagine the opposite of it. Visualise yourself shaking your leg in a chair. Do this activity now. Now, let me give a very different perspective on how you can stop doing these behaviours. For the longest time, you have accepted these behaviours because your brain made you feel that you need some sort of defence mechanisms to protect yourself in a public place. How about every time you have the urge to crack your fingers in public, you do this and whisper this to yourself, take a deep breath and say, **"These behaviours are of no use, stop."** You rewire your brain to make it understand it's new normal which is **embracing nothingness**. Yes, sitting in a chair and doing absolutely nothing is nowadays considered boring, and which is why you can't help it but check your phone even though it's for nothing but scrolling. Your reflex actions are constantly trying to protect you from everything in the environment, but the remote control is in your hands. You can either follow those actions or challenge yourself to do better.

In my 12 years of career of dealing with people in a social setting, what has worked for me and built strong connections during these years is facing the social situation head on. Following are the best five ways to feel better before you enter a social scenario until it becomes a piece of cake for you, and you start enjoying it.

1. **Take three deep breaths-** Inhale from your nose and exhale from your mouth. You can also use the 4-7-8 technique. Inhale counting to four, hold for seven seconds and exhale counting to eight. This will instantly relax you and provide more oxygen to your body and brain to think clear and better.

2. **Look around and get a grip of your environment –** Don't you feel safe at home? Why? Because you are so comfortable with the environment. When you look around, you are making yourself comfortable with your new surroundings, which will eventually make you feel at ease.

3. **Look directly at people and smile-**I understand eye contact can be intimidating for many of you, but challenge yourself and push through it. Think of it this

way, as much as you are worried about people's judgements, they are worried about the same thing too, so initiate ice-breaking by just looking and giving a warm smile to fellow communicators. It will look awkward for three seconds and then becomes the best decision of your life.

4. **Here and now-** It's easy to lose sight of where you are when you are socially awkward. Your mind has a habit of wandering and dreaming about when this is going to end so I can go back to my cocoon. Am I right? That's the time you need to challenge your own thoughts and stay in the moment. Try this easy trick- Count five things you see in your environment, and you will find yourself back in no time.

5. **The Shift-** When I used to be nervous, the one thing that always hindered my growth was using words like "I have to go to this event and talk with people, not sure how am I going to do that'. How about we change the narrative to "This is my chance to remove my inhibitions, it can look nerve-wracking, but I will try my best" What did we do here? We made it an opportunity rather than a task which needs to be done and dusted.

Having said that, try not to take these five warm-ups as "Tasks", take them as something which is making your communication journey easy. Remember, it is about your mindset and nothing else. You have the power in you to take control of your mindset, but we are too hypnotised by distractions in the environment. It's high time you take back your power and use it for good. We have understood the habits that make us look nervous and how to control them.

Now let's learn the ways in which you can ace your non-verbal communication in any setting you go.

1. Don't talk to the floor, it might not respond- I am messing with you, ha-ha. What I mean is, whenever you enter through a door in a room, look parallel to the floor. In fact, look around. Staring at the floor might be easiest way to avoid any possible eye contact, but if you want to make a difference, look up and keep your shoulders relaxed. This is something that I have learnt repetitively when I was modelling. There used to be times when you must look down to see a wobbly ramp, so you don't fall on your face, but we were instructed not to do that as it impacts your overall looks on the ramp. What started as an instruction has now turned into a full-time habit. Looking at people and parallel to the floor not only makes you look confident, but it also adds a lot to your posture which automatically shrugs when no one is looking, which makes you look like a turtle.

2. Be all smiles- You must have heard this, smile, it doesn't cost anything. I want to tell you, it does cost; it costs your presence in a room. Let me get this straight, people like being in the presence of happy and wholesome people. In case, you have been finding that person for a long time, it's you, it's always been you. A simple, warm smile might not get you an award, but it will help in lighting a room, and that's exactly what we are trying to do here. To add more charm, say hello to whoever you see. It breaks the ice and makes you and people around you comfortable.

3. Take it slow and steady- One thing that gets noticed almost instantly in public is how fast your actions are. Making a shift entry and then rushing your small actions, like sitting on a chair in a hurry, and looking like a crow here and there, make you perceive anxiety (did you just visualise a crow?). Instead, take your sweet time to do the smallest tasks, as if you have no care in the world. A secret- People like people who bring peace and calmness to their personalities, and doing things at your own pace is a beautiful foundation for building one.

4. If blood is not on your hands, try not to hide them- Now, this is an easy mistake that we unknowingly do in public without realising it. But hey! It's totally natural. Your reflex actions are always protecting you. We must rewire our brains to feel normal doing nothing with our hands. Keep them in front and try not to stuff them inside your pockets. Keeping both of your hands in pockets can show disinterest or disrespect to your listener and your audience. Feel free to put one hand with your thumb out if at all you must.

5. The balance- Have you observed your body balance when you are standing? We often find ourselves shifting our body weight from one leg to another. Relatable? You might think it is because of the nervousness, but it is mostly because your body is not standing in a balanced manner. This is how you should do it. Stand with your legs shoulder-length apart, and you will never lose your balance again. If you feel this position is not that comfortable, then you can take your one leg out and keep one straight. This way you even put one of your hands on your straightened leg, and feel comfortable while talking in a standing position.

Non- verbal communication and your body language play a huge role in gauging your confidence. Always remember, confidence is silent, and insecurities are loud. If you have ever confused loudness with confidence, it's high time you challenge yourself. Bring out the calmness in you and confidence will get along automatically. Non-verbal communication is a huge topic, but the above learnings are more than enough for you to work in the next year to get started with your body language journey. Your body do the talking more than your mouth does, so make it count.

Chapter - 4

Building Rapport and Connection: The Heart of Effective Communication

I need you to think about any latest gathering you were in and hold a conversation with someone on a deeper level. What do you remember from that conversation that can confirm that you made a connection with them? Finding things that were common, perhaps? Or tiny things about them made you feel instantly at home? That's the thing about building connections with people. People who felt like a cozy hug in your life are usually the people who made you feel comfortable about your vulnerabilities. Am I right?

Imagine building relationships with people like nurturing a plant. It needs food, water, and prompt care for it to grow. It's easy to just create a connection, but to nurture it, it requires work which needs to be put in consistently. Let me ask you a simple question, when you visit a doctor to cure any health problems you are facing, do you trust the doctor that he will give the right medicine for you? I am hoping your answer is yes. So, when you get cured by their medication, you always visit the same doctor for any health issues because now you have complete trust in him or her. Do you agree that it's a form of connection? Yes, it is. Let's dive deep into the intricacies of making genuine connections with people.

1- **Be interested-** When you are new to communicating with people, one of the biggest worries we all have is that we want to sound interesting to the other person. I hate to break this to you; it does not matter. What really matters in a conversation is how interested you are in the other person. How to do that you may ask? Listen, just listen. When people are sharing something, be completely present in the moment and be there for them. Don't try to figure out what you are going to say next once they finish. If you focus on listening attentively, you will automatically have things to say. In case you are still worried about your response to them, ask an open-ended question so they can open more. "Are you okay?" only has one answer, "yes or no" but asking "How was your day at work?" Is a thinker and will give your communicator the opportunity to speak more.

2. Try not to conflate experiences-Understand this one simple thing, every single person existing on this planet is different from you on all levels. Your looks, your circumstances, how you feel, what makes you happy, etc. It is only fair for you to not conflate your situation with others and accept them as they are. Which brings me to one of the most important pillars of making connections with people, empathy. There is a fine line between showing sympathy and empathy. Sympathy can sound more like feeling sad for the other person or showing pity. Empathy, on the other hand, is about feeling what the other person is going through and putting yourself in their shoes, genuinely trying to understand their situation without judging them. When you genuinely empathise with the other person, it not only makes them feel safe about sharing something with you, it also builds trust, which is the stepping stone of rapport building.

3- Save your sob stories for another time- This might sound harsh, but let me explain. Imagine you are meeting someone for the first time, and they start telling you stories about how sad they have been for a month and how things are not in their favour. You can say that you will try to empathize as explained in the above point but tell me honestly are you going to meet them again? Probably not. It's okay to share an incident or two about certain setbacks you are facing in life but if your conversation is all about how sad your life is, it is probably going to make the other person think twice about meeting you next. Let's face it, life is not easy, and a lot of people are struggling with something in their own ways and if you are going to throw a rock of sorrow on them for the very first time you meet them, they are definitely going to run away. Save your life and its struggles for later and share them in small chunks. You don't have to fake happiness, that's not what I meant. You can talk about your point of views, your take on things, etc. Instead of oversharing everything in the first meeting.

4- Your niceness won't win you an Oscar- What I mean is, BE REAL. The type of cars you have or the type of house you prefer to live in can add leaves to your social status but will not work in making genuine connections. Real people don't care about materialistic stuff, they care about how things make you feel. No matter how amazing something is for people, speak it out loud if it doesn't sit with you. You don't have to say "that's nice" to everything people say. If it doesn't fit the bill, speak up. You don't have to fight or raise your voice, but a gentle "I disagree" and "here is why" is more than enough to voice your opinion. Remember, being fake nice may get 100 people on your side, but being real will get five authentic ones who support the things that you support. 100 meaningless acquaintances or five real genuine connections, what do you prefer? Stop being nice and start being real.

5- Stay Civil- Whether it's about friendships, relationships, or your parents, if you find yourself being disrespectful to any of them, it's not going to work. Disregard towards other people is the easiest way to lose them. It should neither be done nor be accepted. The simplest way to respect the other person is to acknowledge their viewpoint. Remember what I mentioned in the second point? Life is not the same for everyone and recognising what another person is feeling is the highest form of showing respect and love. I need you to remember the last time you fought with a friend of yours. Was it a disagreement? Did you feel that they did not support you? What if they told you things like, "I understand what you feel, and I am sorry you feel this way, but here is what I am feeling" instead of just putting you off for how you felt? Would that make things a little better? I am assuming your answer is yes. That's exactly what I am talking about. People don't feel hurt about disagreement; they feel hurt about disregard for how they felt about something. Being courteous and respectful towards each other's boundaries will confirm the kind of person you are and if the other person can trust you or not, which is directly proportional to the kind of connections you make.

When you meet someone for the first time it's natural to feel a little uncomfortable as you are still in the process of knowing each other, but try not to misunderstand that initial nervousness into judging yourself about being socially awkward. Let me tell you one simple thing, meeting new people is mostly awkward for everyone. Some people just have better conversational skills than others, and some people are still learning them. If you are the latter, don't judge yourself too harshly. In a few encounters, you will get better too. Here are five things to remember. If you have just started opening yourself to new people and are new to learning communication skills

1. **Try not to rush the process** – It's natural to feel sad when your first attempt fails, but remember that even a simple habit like brushing your teeth before going to bed can take 21 days to settle in. So, talking to new people is extremely nerve-wracking if you're not used to it. Be gentle with yourself in the process of learning how to communicate.

2. **Confidence is not technique, but a process**- A Lot of internet gurus are teaching the techniques to become confident instantly, but building confidence is a journey of its own. It's a muscle that you build over time and strengthen along the way.

3. **Not everyone you meet is going to be kind to you**- Yes. This is one of the most recent lessons that I have learnt. Let's face it, people are mean and insecure, they don't leave a single chance to pass that on to you which ultimately makes you doubt yourself. The punch line is don't let those people decide your self-worth. There are

going to be times when you're going to come home feeling dejected, but trust me, the problem was not yours but how people generally are sometimes, and hey! That's totally fine.

4. **It's okay to say I don't know-** When you're talking to new people one of the most embarrassing things that you will come across again and again is not knowing something. As daunting as it sounds, remember it's better to say you don't have any idea than to pass on wrong information and make a fool of yourself. Confidence is not only about knowing everything. It is also about gracefully accepting when you don't.

5. **Listen to your body-** When something is not sitting with you, especially in the case of meeting new people, believe it. Our body automatically starts creating excuses for discomfort that eventually, it's going to be fine, but alas, it doesn't. Know the difference between initial awkwardness and discomfort. While both might sound the same, they feel different. People can fake it but your body is smart enough to smell it. Trust your gut feelings.

Overall, remember, people might not care about what you were wearing the other day, but they will always remember how you made them feel. Making connections is like playing chess, it requires strategy, foresight, and the willingness to take risks.

Chapter - 5

Overcoming Fear and Anxiety: Confidence in Challenging Situations

When was the last time you spoke in front of people? Can you remember it for me and try to feel how you were feeling when you had to do it? I am assuming you would be choosing words like nervousness, anxiety, and a bit scared before you started it. Those are the body's natural reactions, and even the most popular public speakers in the world face those. When you are in a situation which is unfamiliar to your body, you naturally start to feel such emotions. The problem is, we start to take them too close to our hearts, and instead of training ourselves to manage them, we repetitively find ourselves stuck and getting cold feet. Let's get this one thing out of the window. Every emotion that you feel has the full potential to be used as a tool to grow and not a threat to your self-esteem. Let's break them into pieces and give you a 360-degree view of understanding and managing those emotions and feeling more confident.

1. **Changing the narrative-** To overcome anything, you need to first acknowledge it. I understand that you must be wondering, "But I just confessed that I was nervous" but, if you want to grow out of it, you need to change the narrative of your acknowledgment from "I feel nervous when I publicly speak" to "I understand I am nervous and that is ok." The power of words and how self-assurance can literally be done without external

validation. The idea is to be extremely gentle with yourself in such situations. You know how superheroes magically appear and save the day? How about you become your own superhero and save yourself? The best way to start that is by changing how you talk to yourself. Your narrative with yourself is directly proportional to the narrative of others with you.

2. **Understanding the root cause-** Now, as much as you are tempted to tell me that it's because there are a lot of people and that is what makes me nervous, I hate to break it to you that is not 100% accurate in most of the circumstances. Fear of being in public is rooted in your insecurities. Ask yourself, what goes in my mind when I stand in front of an audience? I can guarantee that most of us start worrying about "how am I looking?" "What if this goes badly?" "Are people going to judge me?" "Am I looking fat? Are people going to start talking about that?" "How am I going to sound?" I can see you are nodding your head. While these thoughts are normal, worrying about what people are thinking is an absolute waste of time. Yes, people might think about that, but how far would you like to go with that thought? Don't you think it's going to drive you crazy? The idea is to start working on your insecurities. Whatever you think that you don't feel confident about, start working on it. Once your competence increases, your confidence increases too.

3. **Practise mindfulness-** Mindfulness is the art of staying in the moment. Our brain has the tendency to go on a world tour when it is put on the spot, but you are fully

capable of pulling it back to the current moment. Anxiousness is rooted in worrying about what is going to happen. I need you to shift your focus to "what is happening right now." The easiest way to do that in a public speaking scenario is to make eye contact with people which will put you at ease almost instantly. Take a moment to absorb where you are and what is happening instead of worrying about the future.

4. **Focus on what you can control-** It's easy to lose sight of what really matters in high pressure situations like public speaking or having a conversation with strangers. We tend to focus on things beyond our control like audiences' reactions and making a good impression, but reality is far away from it. To make you feel even better, here is a list of things that can be controlled.

Your Preparation – Either for a speech or a conversation with new people, prepare.

Your Opening- Most of our nervousness stays dominant for the first few minutes. Practise your opening as many times as you have to get it right. Trust me, a good start saves the day.

Your body language- Stand tall and maintain an open posture. This conveys confidence and authority, even if you're feeling nervous.

Breathing-Nervousness can lead to shallow or rapid breathing. Focus on taking deep, steady breaths before and during your speech to help you stay calm and control your voice.

Mindset- Shift your focus away from worrying about how you're being perceived and focus on delivering your message.

Handling Mistakes- Acknowledge and move on if you make a mistake, acknowledge it briefly and keep moving. Don't let small errors throw you off. Most of the time, the audience won't notice unless you draw attention to it.

A solid mindset shift can lead to great results. Remember, anything can be achieved with a mindset that acknowledges their strengths and mistakes and is committed to growing. Anxiety and nervousness are part of the process of becoming confident, and instead of beating yourself up about why you feel a certain way, surrender to it and focus more on finding solutions.

Chapter - 6
Developing Assertiveness: Setting Boundaries and Expressing Needs

I was watching an interview of a 90-year-old author who looked super young. The journalist wanted to know her beauty secret, and she said "boundaries". She further added, "Nothing ages you more than people running all over your boundaries". I come from the early 90's, and I learned this word five years ago. Shocking right? I don't think my parents ever asked me to say a stiff "no" to situations in which I did not feel comfortable. More than saying, I believe we have never been taught about how to say no. People pleasing is our natural state of being, and "I don't want to hurt your feelings" has become our mantra. Let's break it today, shall we? We have spent enough time thinking about other people's feelings. Let's learn how to not hurt your own feelings, which you happily give up on most of the occasions.

What are boundaries?

Boundaries are limits you set for yourself and others regarding what is acceptable behaviour in various situations. They protect your time, energy, emotions, and values. Setting a boundary is not a luxury or an option, this must become a default setting within you. If you find it difficult to say no and have felt guilty doing it, it's time to strengthen your boundaries.

Types of Boundaries

1. **Emotional Boundaries:** Protect your feelings and personal space.
2. **Physical Boundaries:** Define how much physical space you need and your comfort with touch.
3. **Mental Boundaries:** Respect your thoughts, opinions, and beliefs.
4. **Time Boundaries:** Manage your time by knowing when to say no and prioritising commitments.

The real challenge of setting a boundary is learning how to express it to people? Saying no with a poker face might come across as rude or cold and which is why you need to learn this word "assertiveness." Assertiveness is the ability to express your opinions, feelings, and needs in a direct, honest, and respectful way. If you know how to assertively communicate, your relationships get better, your self-esteem increases, and ultimately you are less stressed, and as a result, you are more confident.

As I keep reminding you of the importance of understanding a problem's root cause. Why do you think you struggle with setting boundaries and saying no? It is again rooted in your insecurities. Here are three major reasons.

Fear of Rejection: Many people fear that being assertive will lead to rejection or conflict. This fear can lead to passivity, where you avoid speaking up for your needs to avoid disapproval.

Cultural or Upbringing Factors: Some cultures or family dynamics discourage assertiveness, leading to difficulties in setting boundaries. If you were raised to always please others, you might feel uncomfortable asserting yourself.

Confusing Assertiveness with Aggression: Many people avoid assertiveness because they equate it with being rude or confrontational. It's important to recognize that assertiveness, unlike aggression, is respectful of both your needs and the needs of others.

Now let's make you assertive.

What does the nation want? - I mean, start by being clear about what you want or need in each situation. Assertiveness begins with understanding and acknowledging your own desires and limits.

Stop with the "you" game and start with "I" game- We have the tendency to blame others when our needs are not met. For example, "you always give me too much work." How about we change it to "I feel overwhelmed when I have too many responsibilities."

NO means NO- One of the most important aspects of assertiveness is learning to say no without feeling guilty. Start small and gradually increase your comfort with declining requests that don't align with your priorities.

Keep calm- If you find it difficult to say no, there is a high chance that you will automatically become aggressive. That's where the real challenge lies. Keep a relaxed posture and the tone of your voice. Focus on being clear and neutral.

Setting Boundaries in Different Areas of Life

Don't get personal- Have a friend who's never on time and you, being a punctual pumpkin always suffers? Setting boundaries in personal relationships ensures that your emotional needs are met while maintaining mutual respect. For example, if a friend constantly oversteps your time, kindly but firmly expresses your need for space. If they don't understand, you know what to do.

Workplace boundaries- has **"sure sir"** always been your go-to word at the workplace and you look forward to a tea break because you are biting off more than you can chew? Assertiveness at work is crucial for avoiding burnout and maintaining professionalism. Set boundaries with colleagues or managers by clearly defining your workload and priorities. Politely decline tasks that are beyond your capacity or unrelated to your role.

What's your Insta? - Having a phone in your hand all the time doesn't necessarily affirm that you are always available. In today's world, it's essential to set boundaries with technology and social media. Be clear about your availability for work emails, texts, or social interactions, and don't be afraid to disconnect when necessary.

To be married to the idea of setting a boundary, you need to get this

Be patient- Assertiveness is a skill that develops over time. Be consistent in practicing it, even in small interactions. The more often you assert yourself, the more natural it will become.

How did you feel? After setting boundaries or asserting yourself, take time to reflect. What worked? What felt challenging? This reflection helps you adjust and improve your communication.

How was I- Ask trusted friends or mentors for feedback on your assertiveness. They can offer valuable insights on how you're coming across and where you might improve.

Chances of you still feeling guilty are high, and which is why you need to understand this.

Setting a boundary or being assertive is not selfish but an act of preserving your well-being. Remember, you must have the RIGHT to express your needs to others. I understand that our wiring has been done in a very different way and these concepts are alien to you. Be gentle with yourself. I remember when I said my first "no", I started crying and shaking. Do not feel demotivated when you are uncomfortable. Your road to being super comfortable with your life might look and feel uneasy, it's not easy to break old habits but trust me, this one will be totally worth it!

Chapter - 7

Adapting Communication Styles: Flexibility for Different Audiences

Have you ever felt like your message is not understood by everyone? The most common statement used by people when they are not able to express themselves in a specific situation is "you just don't get it." And although some part of it is dependent on whether the person in front of you can understand your message, mostly it is dependent on how you are communicating that message. Let's understand this one thing, you have full freedom to change your way of communicating depending on what situation demands. You may see me with the most humble and sweetest tone with the people I trust and adore, but the moment I see something fishy my tone changes. Effective communication is not one-size-fits-all. The ability to adapt your style based on the audience you're speaking to is a key trait of successful communicators.

The Importance of Adaptability in Communication

- **But why?-** Adapting your communication style is essential because different people interpret and respond to messages in unique ways. Your tone, vocabulary, body language, and message delivery should shift depending on who you are speaking to—whether it's a formal presentation to a corporate team or a casual chat with friends.

- **Connect more-** When you tailor your communication, you're more likely to build trust and understanding with your audience. It demonstrates empathy and respect for their perspective and makes your message more relatable.

- **Improving Your Influence-** Flexibility allows you to connect with people on a deeper level, making it easier to influence decisions, change perspectives, or resolve conflicts.

Now let's make your job easier by understanding when, how, and why you need to alter your communication style.

Who are we speaking to? - Notice how we need to talk in a certain way to a newborn baby? They don't understand our language. They respond to a different frequency, and you don't get upset about that, so why with people? You need to change the way of communicating according to the age, education, profession, and cultural background of the person. Yes, all this matters.

How much do they know?- Not everyone is on the same page that you are currently reading. You are about to confidently communicate, and the person who you might be communicating with in the future, might not even be aware about this book. It's not necessary that people you communicate with know as much as you do and vice-versa. You should tailor your communication according to how much a person is aware of things you are talking about. If they're experts, you can use technical jargon; if they're beginners, break things down into simpler terms.

What's the end game? - Every conversation you make has a meaning and purpose. If you know the purpose of your conversation and what you should gain out of it, this helps you craft it accordingly and set aside unrealistic expectations. For example, if you talk to your parents and expect them to be happy and cheerful about the things only your friends understand, it's unfair for your parents to provide. You need to speak to them according to what they expect from you. Try not to be single-minded in your approach.

Different people demand different styles of communications. Depending on where they are coming from, you should tailor your style.

- **Too direct?-** Some audiences prefer direct, straightforward communication, while others might find this approach too aggressive. In cultures or settings where indirect communication is valued, be mindful of using subtle cues and non-verbal signals.

- **Emotionally Driven vs. Fact Based** - Some people are more persuaded by emotional stories, while others rely on data and facts. Use emotional appeals when addressing a more empathetic audience and rely on statistics and logic when dealing with analytical thinkers.

Now, even if you take care of the points above and try your best to adapt to a style your listener would appreciate, there are still chances of you being misinterpreted. Careful curation of words can still go wrong if:

You and your body language are not in sync- sometimes, your body language or tone may not match the message you're trying to send. Stay aware of your non-verbal communication and adjust based on your audience's reaction. If they seem confused or disengaged, shift your approach.

Don't check personality type- Extroverts may respond well to lively, energetic communication, while introverts might prefer a calm and measured approach. Be flexible enough to adjust based on who you're interacting with.

Don't forget!

To be you- While it's important to adapt your communication, don't lose your authenticity. Be flexible but stay true to your core values and voice. Authenticity resonates with all audiences and builds trust.

Having a flexible approach to your communication is not only a powerful and smart way to deal with people, but also a recipe for a stress-free life. We communicate too much about ourselves, but it's about your audience or who you are speaking to. Whether you're speaking to a room of executives or having a casual chat with friends, your ability to adjust your message will set you apart as a confident, empowered communicator.

Chapter - 8
Confidence in Public Speaking: Owning the Stage

Public speaking is not for everyone. Whoever has said this needs to be grounded forever. It's not a big deal and can be done by everyone, if you learn to just get out of your head and get in the moment. According to me, public speaking is a combination of mastering three things. Exposure + Working on your insecurities + Being in the moment. Let's unravel these one by one.

1. Exposure- Remember the first foundation of confidence? Yes, it's exposure. You CANNOT save yourself from it. If you are planning to become good at public speaking, you must expose yourself to public speaking opportunities diligently as much as you can. Now, as much as I am tempted to suggest to you my top five suggestions to get started on your journey, I would like to introduce you to this little exercise you would like to get started right away. It's not feasible for everyone to join a course or club at times, and which is why this will work for you beautifully. I call it "21 days to stardom". We all have heard of writing down our thoughts daily on a piece of paper, but have you ever tried speaking to them out loud? Yes, I am talking about video journaling. It's like speaking to your therapist friend but without interruption *wink*. Here is what you need to do.

Step- 1- Record yourself for 21 days every day for 3-5 minutes (even longer if you would like). Look directly into the camera lens and imagine that you are talking to someone who has just asked you, how was your day and how did you feel today?

Step-2- Play the video after 15 minutes (I will tell you why) and don't look at it. Just listen.

Step-3- Play the video one more time, but this time on mute.

Step-4- Make a Google Drive folder and upload these videos every day for the next 21 days.

Let's understand how this activity helps you become a better speaker

When you record yourself daily for 21 days you get comfortable expressing yourself without making a conversation. It's a different experience than just talking to people.

21 days help you in creating a habit. Remember, habit is everything. Once something becomes a part of your daily, life, it becomes a piece of cake eventually. How do you think seasoned speakers have become so confident? It has kind of become their everyday job.

When you just listen to yourself, you get comfortable with your vocal image. How are you sounding? Do you like listening to yourself? If not, this is your chance. You cannot change your natural voice, but you can always enhance it with various vocal exercises. The idea is to make peace with the way your voice comes across.

When you look at yourself speaking you get comfortable with your visual image. How do you look when you speak? It's not about your physique. It's about how you move when you speak. What is your body language when you are speaking, are you moving too much or not at all? How are your hands moving or are they not moving at all? What are your facial expressions? Are you energetic enough, or is it looking dull?

The reason I asked you to wait for 15 minutes before looking at your video is because we have the habit of judging ourselves too hard, especially when you're going to create videos for the first time.

This might not take you more than 10-15 minutes, but I guarantee that you will start feeling better once you complete it. Please note:

Your entire body is visible when you are recording.

You speak louder than your natural volume.

Make sure there is no one disturbing you for these minutes.

Create a diary and write everyday what you need to improve the next day.

Checklist for a good speaker

- You are audible
- You are clear
- You are not rushing
- You are moving your hands and not keeping them stuck
- You are not stuck at one place and are moving around

- You keep your energy high.

Remember, this is just a starter for you to get things moving. Here are my top five suggestions to expose yourself to public speaking.

1. Join a Public Speaking Group (e.g., Toastmasters)

- **Why**: Toastmasters and similar organisations provide a structured, supportive environment for practicing public speaking. You'll get regular opportunities to speak, receive feedback, and improve your skills.
- **How**: Look for local chapters or online meetings to join. Attend regularly to build comfort and confidence.

2. Volunteer to Speak at Work or School

- **Why**: Offering to present at meetings, lead discussions, or give briefings helps you gain experience in familiar environments. It's a low-pressure way to practise public speaking with an audience you already know.
- **How**: Raise your hand for presentation opportunities, volunteer to lead workshops, or organise team updates.

3. Attend and Speak at Networking Events or Conferences

- **Why**: Networking events often have open mic sessions or panels where attendees can share ideas, introduce themselves, or discuss a topic. Conferences also offer opportunities to present, whether it's a short speech or a panel discussion.
- **How**: Attend industry-specific networking events, apply to be a speaker or panelist, or offer to present at community events.

4. Start a YouTube Channel or Podcast

- **Why**: Creating content force you to practise delivering messages clearly and confidently in front of a camera or microphone. It's a great way to build public speaking skills while reaching a broad audience.

- **How**: Begin by recording short videos or podcasts on topics you're passionate about. As you get more comfortable, increase the length or complexity of your presentations.

5. Host or Present Webinars/Workshops

- **Why**: Webinars and online workshops allow you to practise public speaking in a virtual setting, where you can deliver educational or informative content to an audience.

- **How**: Create a workshop or training session around a skill you excel in. Partner with organisations or platforms to host it or do it independently through social media or professional networks.

These strategies will help you develop confidence while gaining valuable speaking experience in various settings.

2. **<u>Working on your insecurities</u>-** Let me get this one thing out of your head. Even the most confident communicators are insecure about one thing or another. Nobody is perfect. When you present yourself on stage, it's more than natural to feel nervous about yourself. People go in all directions in their heads when they have been put on the spot, especially if it's a public speaking opportunity. Here are few things you need to remember when you feel insecure about yourself.

What makes you feel this way? -Understand the root cause of everything that you are feeling. For example-

Insecurity-Are people going to make fun of my looks?

Root cause-Are you insecure about what you are wearing or how does your body look?

Solution-Do I need to work on my styling, or do I need to work out?

And this is how you simplify your insecurities. When you know what you need to work on, you instantly start to feel better.

Find Evidence for your insecurities- The moment you thought of a limiting belief, for example- "I am not good at public speaking" immediately ask yourself, What proof do I have in this moment that can support that? Most of you will find nothing because there is no evidence that exists anywhere. Once that happens, replace it with a constructive one- "I am going to be fine."

Slow and steady- If you are new to learning public speaking, the chances of you not being good at it for the first 3-5 times are very high, so do not jump to an audience of 50 or above. Start with just three-four people. Ask your family or friends to support you and become your audience, and then gradually increase the number of people.

I love you - Yes, I do! But you need to show some love to yourself too, especially during these times. The worst thing that you can do to yourself is wait for external validation about how amazing you are. Treat those compliments as a bonus, and not something that decides your self-worth.

Congratulations for reading this book and finally starting to work on your communication skills. Now go and make yourself your favourite beverage and enjoy it with some music. And that's how you celebrate small wins. Not just for this book, do it on a daily basis, and acknowledge your strengths.

3. **Being in the moment** – Now, this concept is alien to a lot of people, but 'Mindfulness' has the capability to solve 99% of your problems. You may ask, how? Our brain has the tendency to go in the past and the future almost all the time, and that's how anxiety is born. But if you stay in the moment, you will be shocked to realise that you have no thoughts running and you are at peace. Imagine feeling this peace throughout the day. You feel mindfulness when you are indulged in a really good conversation with someone or having fun with your friends. You are happy and at peace because, IN those moments, you were 'in the moment. Here is how you become mindful before a public speaking opportunity.

Yogic breathing- Equal amount of inhalation and exhalation.

Feel the surface – Acknowledge where you are standing or sitting and touch it to feel grounded.

Quick smiles- Look at someone in the audience and smile. This will relax you almost instantly.

Remember, when you indulge yourself in learning a new skill, be extremely patient with yourself. Try not to be too quick and rush to make judgements. It takes months and years to become a master at something. Be gentle and show yourself the love you deserve, even during the process. If you embrace the process, you will enjoy the outcome even more.

Chapter - 9

Handling Criticism and Feedback: Turning Challenges into Growth Opportunities

It's easier said than done, but when someone talks to you about your weak points, it's easy to be dragged into self-criticism. We personally have never been taught to take feedback constructively, nor do we work smartly towards it. When you are on a journey to become good at something, you are going to be bad at it in the initial phases. So, when you know you are going to learn it eventually, why beat yourself up when someone directly says it?

It's not about you- When you communicate, you're often sharing thoughts, feelings, or professional ideas. It can feel personal when others criticise these expressions, but recognising that feedback is about your approach, not your worth, is key.

You should join defence- because you are so good at it. I know I need to crack better jokes, but you also need to be open about it. Get it? *wink*. What I am trying to say is, start being open and stop being defensive. A mindset shift is all we need here. Life is a continuous learning process. Understand that this is important for you to be better at it and it's not a threat to your self-worth.

Remove Reacting from your dictionary – as it hardly helps. You need to start responding. Reaction is a reflex action but responding is a conscious choice. Take some deep breaths, think about what is being said and then make an opinion.

Here are some simple techniques to follow when you are being criticised or receiving feedback.

There is a reason you have two ears- So you listen more. Don't even try to interrupt when someone is giving you feedback because in the fit of rage, you might do that and miss a chance to be complimented. Not everyone is planning a conspiracy against you, maybe they are just trying to help? Try to keep that approach in mind and stay calm.

But what if they are planning a conspiracy? – Mostly not, but not everyone knows how to give feedback, so they abruptly tell you things and try to escape. There is a possibility that they might not hold your best interest, so don't just sit quietly and accept a vague comment like "I felt your tone was off." Ask them what exactly they meant by that and what all you need to improve.

Pause- Not from reading this book, my friend, but before you respond to that feedback. Remember this simple rule, anything that instantly comes from your mouth in response to something is mostly not going to be right and will be led by your emotions. Breathe-Reflect-Respond. Make this your new mantra and thank me later.

Now that we know how to receive feedback, let's use it as a tool for your growth.

Focus on the 'what' and not 'how'- the feedback is delivered. Even though people need to focus on how they say things and not what they say, you as a receiver need not worry about that or take it close to your heart. Focus on the message, not on the delivery.

Apply immediately – As tempted as you feel to respond to the feedback, try to channel that energy into practicing it and making it better. If someone said you were speaking too fast, practise speaking slow and nail it in your next opportunity.

Understand your audience- Feedback will also help you in understanding what works for whom. Your tonality and style might work for one person and not for another. Adapt accordingly.

Feedback is a great way to become a better version of yourself. While going through this journey of growth and development, remember these three things so you never feel disappointed.

You are not your communication skills- Remember, it's a skill and it needs its own time to develop. Separate yourself from your skills. Criticism of your communication style isn't criticism of you as a person. This separation helps you handle feedback more objectively and use it constructively.

Empathise- I understand not all intentions are right and true, but mostly in the case of feedback, the underlying intention is to help you improve. Practicing empathy and understanding the intention behind feedback can help you stay calm and focused on growth.

Don't forget to give yourself some extra love - Every living creature on this planet makes mistakes. Don't be too harsh on yourself. Practise self-compassion. Be kind to yourself when receiving feedback, recognising that it's part of the learning process.

Handling criticism and feedback is tricky. Chances are high that you are going to forget the advice above. If you are not able to apply these learnings the very first time you are in a feedback session, it's TOTALLY ok. There is always a second time and a third time perhaps. It's never too late. When you successfully do it for the first time, send me a celebratory email.

Chapter - 10

Maintaining Confidence Long-Term: Strategies for Sustainable Communication.

I remember working for a Bangalore-based company as their official anchor to represent their Hindi YouTube channel, and it was my first day of shooting a video. I was confident that I could handle it easily, as the camera is something that comes naturally to me. After 15 minutes of trying to shoot the introduction, I asked the camera person to give me a 10-minute break. I could not do it the way I imagined it. You know why? Because I stopped practicing, and I was facing the camera almost after two years. The only reason I finished it, after all, is because I believe in my capabilities. But was it my best work? No. That's the thing about confidence and communication. Firstly, you are not born with these traits, it's a skill. Secondly, a skill can only be mastered if you keep enhancing it over the period. You can't magically feel confident if you do not work on it every single day. Here is what you need to remember if you want to start your journey of confidence and make it sustainable. These are non-negotiables.

Believe in yourself

Instead of focusing on what your weak points are, focus on your strengths. You must remind yourself of your capabilities and strengths every day. Take time to recognize what you do well, whether it's being a good listener, having clear articulation, or being emotionally intelligent. A critical aspect of maintaining confidence is a deep understanding of your strengths as a communicator.

Don't be afraid of challenges. Remember, challenges are going to be there no matter what you do. They are not the end of the world. When you slowly walk through life with this perspective, you will realise that that was the only way to grow. It will not be easy when you experience them, but never forget they are tools for your personal development, and not a threat to your identity.

How to stay consistent

Regular exposure is the key- Write down how many times in a week or month you need to publicly speak to feel natural about it. Volunteer to speak at office meetings or college presentations, etc. to hone your skills. No matter how uncomfortable you feel, push your limits because that is where the real confidence lies.

Work on small, achievable goals- If you are on your journey to become a confident communicator, remember that there are multiple aspects of it. You can't master all the aspects in one go. Break them down into your weekly and monthly goals and work on them accordingly. This gives less anxiety and adds a lot to your confidence.

Adapting to uncertainty is the key

Confidence is not about achieving success; it's about knowing that you can handle every situation with poise and grace. You can't predict the type of audience you are going to get or the type of people you are going to find so you should always be prepared and flexible. The fear of the unknown should not let you down, no matter what.

Life is unpredictable and not everything will go as planned. Develop the ability to think on your feet. Face as many people as you can. Talk to people from all walks of life. Read books and articles and try to understand people's perspectives about life. This will widen your ability to respond.

How do you talk to yourself?

Have you ever observed how you talk to yourself throughout the day, especially when you are going through a tough time. Believe it or not, but talking to yourself with a balanced approach where you understand that it's okay to go through challenges and you will handle it no matter what. This mindset will take your confidence to the next level. The way you talk to yourself will determine how people are going to speak to you. The less nonsense you tolerate, the more confident you become.

Do you envision success?

If you can't see it happening for yourself, how on earth are you going to MAKE it happen? Regularly visualise yourself communicating confidently in various settings. This mental rehearsal helps condition your brain for success, making confident communication feel more natural and attainable in real-life situations.

Maintaining a physical and mental well-being for long lasting success

There is nothing better than feeling physically and mentally fit. You can't deny the fact that the days you looked and felt your best were your most confident days. This is the reason why you need to constantly prioritise exercising. Working out 30 minutes every day can significantly enhance the way you look and feel. Eating wholesome meals with a mindset of nurturing your body is a sustainable way to feel confident about yourself. Checking in with yourself on a regular basis with the help of therapy, coaching, journaling, or talking to a genuine friend about your setbacks and challenges helps in maintaining good mental health.

Practical Techniques for Long-Term Confidence

1. The "Five-Minute Prep" Technique

- Before any major communication event, whether it's a presentation, meeting, or conversation, spend five minutes visualising your success. Picture yourself speaking confidently, maintaining eye contact, and receiving positive reactions. This short burst of visualisation helps condition your mind for success.

2. The "Power Pose"

- Adopt a "power pose" for two minutes before important speaking engagements. Stand tall, with your feet shoulder-width apart and arms spread confidently. This practise helps reduce stress hormones and boosts feelings of confidence, allowing you to approach the situation with self-assurance.

3. Practise the "Elevator Pitch" Daily

- Developing a concise, clear elevator pitch about yourself or your work helps you articulate your thoughts under pressure. Practising it regularly can boost your confidence in everyday conversations and professional settings. Test it out with friends or peers and refine it over time.

4. "Stress-Release Breathing" Technique

- Use a simple breathing exercise to calm nerves before speaking. Inhale for four counts, hold for four counts, exhale for four counts, and repeat. This technique activates the parasympathetic nervous system, reducing stress and boosting confidence.

5. Recording Yourself

- Record your speeches, presentations, or even conversations, and review them. Watching yourself helps you notice areas for improvement and gives you a chance to see your strengths. Over time, you'll develop greater confidence by refining your skills.

Remember, confidence is all about constantly pushing yourself out of your comfort zones and working on becoming your biggest cheerleader. There are going to be days when you will feel miserable even after trying your best. On those days, remind yourself that your worst days do not determine who you are and what you can become. After walking through life's ups and downs in the last 13 years, one thing is for sure, good things take time, and the days you are going to feel like giving up are the days which will motivate you to write a book.

www.ingramcontent.com/pod-product-compliance
Lightning Source LLC
LaVergne TN
LVHW041633070526
838199LV00052B/3337